AF382625

CHOOSING A PROFESSIONAL COACH

Get the guidance that meets your needs

Written by Julie Arcoulin
Translated by Emma Hanna

Coaching 50MINUTES.com

CHOOSING A PROFESSIONAL COACH

- **Problem:** how can I choose the coach who is best suited to my personality and needs?
- **Uses:** finding the right coach is essential in order to ensure that you receive high-quality, effective professional support.
- **Professional context:** personal development, professional wellbeing, professional support.
- **FAQs:**
  - Will an older coach be more qualified than someone younger?
  - Does my success depend entirely on my coach?
  - What are the differences between a coach, a counsellor and a therapist?
  - Can anyone become a coach?
  - What qualities does an effective coach need?
  - Will it be very expensive to hire a good coach?
  - How can I spot a bad coach?

In recent years, there has been a boom in the coaching sector. Supply and demand have shot through the roof, and today there are coaches available for any situation: nutritional coaches, personal development coaches, lifestyle coaches, sports coaches, career coaches, academic coaches – and the list goes on. It is getting more and more difficult to know where to look, never mind how to find a coach who is perfectly suited to our needs. The good news is that with such a wide selection to choose from, it seems statistically implausible that your ideal coach is not out there somewhere. However, that still leaves the question of how to find them, and it can also be all too easy to fall into the trap of hiring a coach who, for one reason or another, is totally unsuited to your needs.

> "During the course of my career, I once came into contact with a man who wanted to work on his relationships with women. During his first session with me, we discussed the fact that he was still in mourning after being widowed, and he admitted that I reminded him of his late wife. It would have been difficult to continue coaching him after that!" (Julie, professional coach)

There are many factors to consider once you decide to hire a professional coach, but the human dimension is the most important of these aspects – after all, coaching is first and foremost a personal issue. Each coach will have their own style (direct, distant, emotional, etc.) and preferred way of doing things. It is up to you to figure out which of these styles will suit you best, with the help of this short book. In just 50 minutes, you will get a full overview of the qualities any good coach must possess, the questions you should ask yourself and the traps to avoid so that you can pick the right coach for the job.

CHOOSING YOUR COACH: THE BASICS

PROFESSIONAL COACHING 101

What does a coach's job involve?

In this context, the word "coach" refers to a person who provides support and advice to an individual as they strive towards professional and/or personal fulfilment. As such, coaching is always envisioned as part of a metaphorical journey. The pace of this journey is set by the client, while the coach provides guidance, motivation and an unshakable belief in their client's potential and eventual success. Coaching is a process which helps the beneficiary to:

- get to know themselves better;
- develop their potential;
- regain their confidence;
- value their abilities;
- set short- and long-term goals.

Coaching is a career in its own right, and has its

own rules, ethics, training and demands. Coach and client work together to identify the obstacles and hindrances the client is facing and to help them draw on their own resources to better meet their goals.

The coaching process

It is helpful to have a good grasp of the coaching process in order to understand its role and what it involves. Generally speaking, it has three stages.

The coaching process

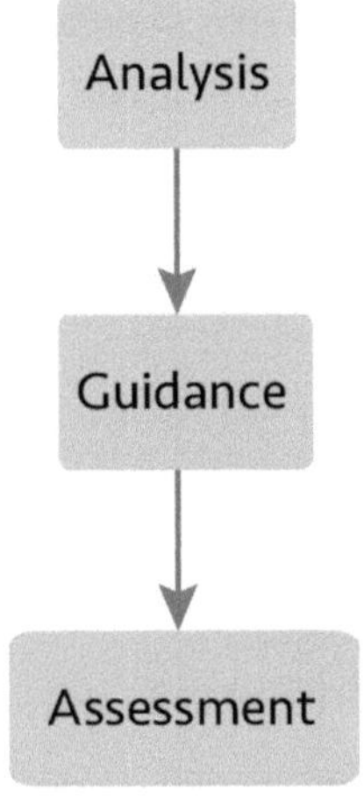

- **Analysis** is the initial phase for laying the groundwork. It involves going over how things currently stand in your professional life and identifying areas for change or improvement. This stage is also the time when you should define your objectives, which is no simple matter. In fact, it often turns out that one of your aims is concealing an underlying motivation. The coach will be there to help you focus on the most precise target possible and then to guide you as you follow this path.
- **Guidance** is the heart and soul of coaching. During this stage, both parties must focus on the goal at hand while also remaining open to any potential changes or developments in the client's needs.

> "One day, I had a consultation with a man in his 40s who wanted to move to live in in the countryside and get away from it all. We started the coaching process with that goal in mind, but as we progressed, it soon became clear that what he really needed was time alone to regain his inner balance and which he could spend however he wanted. As such, we re-evaluated our goal and adjusted our strategies accordingly." (Julie, professional coach)

- **Assessment** is carried out at the end of the coaching process and constitutes an analysis of everything that has been accomplished. No matter whether the result is positive or negative, the coach will always congratulate their client on the progress they have made and encourage them to keep trying to improve.

HOW SHOULD YOU CHOOSE A COACH?

Define your expectations before hiring anyone

Before throwing yourself into the coaching experience, you need to ask yourself the right questions, as your answers will lead you towards a coach with the necessary skills to handle your situation.

- **What are your needs?** Start by identifying which aspects of your life you want to change and the reasons why you are seeking help to do so. Do you simply want someone to confide in? Do you no longer find your job satisfying and want to change career? Do you lack professional motivation? Do you want to improve your self-confidence? Are you looking for financial or legal advice? For example, in the last case you may actually need a legal expert rather than a coach. Identifying your needs – which may be personal as well as professional in nature – is a critical step which will allow you to establish exactly what action you need to take in order to fulfil them.

- **What are your expectations?** Before starting work with a coach, take the time to identify some of the benefits you hope to gain from it. This will allow you to lay out and clarify your current situation, and then to sketch out a course of action which will help you to stay on track during your coaching. Setting clear expectations is also a way of setting a goal; having identified your needs, ask yourself in what specific ways a coach could help you. For example, if your needs are purely professional in nature and are along the lines of "I want to get a new job", "I want to get a raise" or "I want to start my own business", you should look for a coach who is an expert in those areas.

- **Are you prepared to change?** This is the question that really cuts to the heart of the matter, because by engaging the services of a coach, you will be exposing yourself to doubts, transformations, realisations, disappointments, and maybe even the discovery of hidden talents. One thing is certain: afterwards, you will not be the same person. If you have doubts about this, discuss them with your coach during the preliminary interview so that you can determine whether or not the time is right for you to begin coaching.

How can you find a good coach?

- **Word of mouth:** when you make the decision to find a coach, ask around, as someone in your circle may know of a good coach, whether personally or by reputation.
- **Networks and directories:** these are often printed in magazines, and can also be found online. You can try searching for a coach in your town or city and get more information about them by visiting their website (which can often be found via online directories).
- **The media:** pay close attention to TV and radio programmes, and to articles and accounts published in newspapers and magazines. These channels are often brimming with experts from all kinds of fields and, generally speaking,

act as a quality indicator.

- **The internet:** although it is a valuable source of all kinds of information, the problem with the internet is that it is not particularly discriminating. Typing "coach + your area" into a search engine will bring up so many results that you might as well be looking for a needle in a haystack. Of course, there is no harm in taking a look, but sifting through the results will take a colossal effort, and remember that the top results will have been suggested based on their relevance, not on the quality of the coach. You can, however, refine your search by comparing a variety of websites.

GOOD COACHES VS. BAD COACHES

The qualities of a good professional coach

Firstly, remember that there is no such thing as a perfect coach: all you need is someone who meets your expectations. In that sense, the list below, which details the qualities a good coach should have, is not exhaustive, as there is no magic formula to suit everyone. As you read through the list, ask yourself what you expect from your coach and what qualities you consider to be essential, as this will give you some leads to follow in your search.

- **Zero judgement:** when you start working with your coach, it is vital that you do not feel as though you are being judged, as this can lead to total deadlock. A good coach knows that there are as many ways to live and think as there are people, and based on that, no one should ever feel free to judge others. If your coach tries to influence you or impose their views on you, you should take that as a warning sign. However, be careful not to confuse "imposing their own views" with "widening the field of possibilities".
- **Widens the scope of possibilities:** as we have already mentioned, there are as many ways of approaching life as there are people. Quite often, we can end up taking a narrow view of things, thus reducing the number of options open to us. One of a coach's main responsibilities is to broaden their client's professional horizons by helping them to adjust their outlook on life, on their relationships, on their job and, above all, on themselves. If your coach takes a

limited view of things, they will not make you aware of the alternatives that are open to you in your career. The key to successful coaching is: "Change your outlook and you will change yourself".

- **A positive attitude:** if you only remember one thing from this list, make sure that this is it! A coach who takes a positive attitude will help you to look on the bright side of any situation. Being positive, or at least constructive, is one of the cornerstones of coaching. This does not mean lulling you into a false sense of security, but rather helping you to accept and weather the most difficult periods of your life. These moments are the best time to take lessons on board so that you do not fall into the same patterns and the same mistakes as you have in the past.
- **Validation:** self-esteem and self-confidence are two irreplaceable pillars in any journey towards personal and professional fulfilment. As such, coaching should start by building up your self-assurance, which involves validating you as a person: celebrating your successes, whether great or small; taking the view that there is no such thing as a failure, only learning

experiences; and teaching you how to be kind to yourself.

> "Every single client I've ever coached has started out with a lack of self-confidence." (Julie, professional coach)

- **Constant training:** although a coach's quality does not depend solely on their qualifications (certain personal traits are essential), they do give the coach a significant base to work from. The right training provides coaches with the tools and techniques they need to act as guides. Like their clients, coaches are on a constant journey towards improvement, and must carry out additional reading and undergo constant training and supervision in order to progress. One of the traps experienced coaches can sometimes fall into is to stop questioning their own knowledge and to think that they have reached a point where improvement is no longer necessary.

- **A code of conduct:** since coaching is not a licensed profession, anyone can claim to be a coach even if they have no training what-soever, and there are no official professional regulations. Each coach should have their own code of conduct that reflects their own ethics. Of course, there are various coaching groups, associations and federations that coaches can pay to join and which draw up common charters of good practice, but this will in no way guarantee a coach's quality; at the end of the day, it all depends on their personal values, so do not hesitate to ask about this subject during the preliminary interview.
- **Putting the client first:** your coach should not be the centre of attention. Of course, they may use their own personal experiences as a way of illustrating their points, but your coach is there for you – to listen to you, react to you,

and interact with you. The goal is not to resolve their personal problems, but to help you make progress. In fact, one of the ways coaching can go wrong is when the coach projects onto their client. This is a defence mechanism whereby the coach unintentionally begins to project their own thoughts, desires and motivations onto their client, which can then influence the client's feelings and personal experience. The coach's subconscious aim is to live vicariously through their client and use them to solve problems that they were unable to solve in their own life, which leads them to focus their discussions and possibly their advice on that. However, there is no need for undue concern – this is a quintessentially human habit that a good coach will be aware of, and will be actively avoiding so as to maintain their impartiality.

PROJECTION

Projection involves seeing qualities in other people which are actually a reflection of ourselves. For example, if someone annoys you because they talk too much and always seem to make themselves the centre of attention, ask yourself if the real reason you are reacting that way is because you wish you could find the courage to express yourself in public, but have repressed that side of yourself. The same principle applies to the qualities we approve of in other people – often, they correspond to aspects of our own personalities that we feel insecure about.

Coaches to avoid

Not all coaches are created equal, and some will be better equipped to meet your needs and expectations than others. However, there are some warning signs to look out for which will tell you if you should beat a hasty retreat:

- you feel uncomfortable around them;
- they judge you or force their own opinions upon you;
- they often run late, mess around on their smartphone, have a snack while listening to you, etc.;
- they accept any goal you suggest at face value, even if it is unethical;

- they adopt a position of superiority, even though successful coaching is always based on equal footing;
- they present themselves as a saviour, acting as though they have the solution to all your problems and can change your life with a click of their fingers – you will be far better off with a coach who approaches your sessions as a joint effort and who will help you unlock your inner potential to solve your own problems, instead of relying on external solutions.

DIFFERENT CLIENTS, DIFFERENT COACHES

Coaching can be help you to solve a great variety of problems, and finding the coach who is best suited to your needs and goals is not always easy. The following case studies should help you to narrow down your options.

Jacqueline, 43, married with two children, special needs teacher

Jacqueline is looking for a career change. She loves teaching, but wants to branch out into another field and add another string to her bow.

However, her goal is still rather nebulous and a lot of factors need to be taken into account. Firstly, she needs to clearly define her goals and get rid of any potential obstacles or impediments, which often stem from thinking too narrowly. In Jacqueline's case, her career change could come in the form of training as a freelancer. This would require her to let go of the false assumption that all freelancers end up bankrupt because of their fluctuating income. To achieve her goal, she needs to find a coach who can help her with her career change while also helping her adjust her mindset, which suggests that she should look for what is known as a life coach, meaning a coach who addresses aspects of their client's personal and professional lives alike.

Didier, 36, single, business manager

Didier wants to move to a different position within his company and become a coach who specialises in providing guidance for managers. As such, he should look for a business coach, as he requires fairly linear guidance: he has a specific goal and does not need comprehensive coaching. If, like Jacqueline, he had been hoping to make a larger-scale career change and adjust his professional trajectory, Didier would also have needed to confront his limiting beliefs. However, because he is starting with a clear goal in mind, professionally-focused coaching should prove sufficient.

Jeanne, 56, in a relationship with three children, in remission

Jeanne was diagnosed with an illness three years ago. The various treatments she received greatly weakened her, but she is now hoping to start afresh and make the most of her life, using her experiences to find greater meaning in her future. In this case, receiving psychological guidance in parallel with her coaching could also be beneficial, if she has not begun it already, unless Jeanne decides to see a coach who is also trained in therapeutic techniques such as:

- solution-focused brief therapy (SFBT), which focuses on solving surface problems rather than addressing the underlying causes;
- emotionally-focused therapy (EFT), which focuses on using the patient's emotions to help them through their problems;

- Gestalt therapy, which focuses on the way people manage their interactions with their environment, and particularly with other people.

Jeanne would work with both her psychologist and her coach to rebuild her life and find new meaning in it. However, the line between coaching and therapy should be clearly defined. If her coach and her therapist were working in parallel, her coaching sessions would aim to push her into taking action and capitalising on her successes, all while building on and making use of the progress she had made in her therapy sessions. Meanwhile, the therapy sessions would be the time for talking, understanding and in-depth analysis.

Sandrine, 17, student

Sandrine is faced with the immense range of possible fields of study she could go into in the years ahead. She is well aware that this decision will influence her future tremendously, but she cannot even figure out which field she wants to go into. In this case, she should look for an academic coach who will help her to pinpoint her talents, wants and needs. These coaches are generally very well informed about all of the academic options on offer and know how to adapt their approach to the needs of the teenage students they work with, speaking their language and providing them with the tools they need.

To ensure that the coaching is constructive, you should select a coach based on your expectations and the coach's area of expertise. If your goals change during the coaching process, you can always transfer to another coach at any time. A good coach knows their own limits, and will not hesitate to refer you to someone who is better equipped to address your needs. Finally, sometimes coaching can lead to fresh frustrations and take unexpected turns, so it is important to choose a coach who inspires confidence in you and in whom you feel comfortable confiding (without treating them like a shrink, of course).

When is it not necessary to look for a coach?

Sometimes, we simply need to take a bit of time and put our pain into words in order to begin the transformation process. A coach can help you to identify these problems, but they will be mostly action-oriented. If you need to talk to someone but you do not yet feel ready to act, psychotherapy or psychoanalysis might be better suited to your needs. Meanwhile, if you are suffering from mental illness (schizophrenia, bipolar disorder, etc.), you should consider speaking to a doctor.

There are also many reasons, both good and bad, to avoid seeking advice: lack of time or money, difficult personal circumstances, etc. However, these excuses often disguise a fear of failure, and even a fear of success on occasion! As such, you should ask your-self what the real reason for your hesitation is. Talk about that with a coach – call one just to see, in case something that surprises you comes up in the interview.

IN CONCLUSION

Coaching is not a process that comes with a set time frame – it can continue indefinitely. There are always new goals, new learning curves, new experiences, and so on. However, some periods of your life will be more difficult than others, and those are the times when you will need a coach. The first thing to do before choosing a coach is to reconcile yourself to the idea of asking for help. This does not mean telling yourself that you are incapable of handling things on your own, but that your lack of self-confidence and the doubts you are experiencing could lead to failure. This is where a coach comes in, by opening your eyes to the extent of your potential.

Your coach will motivate you, push you, console you, support you, congratulate you, help you to overcome obstacles, and give you a new perspective on everything around you. Coaching is not always a pleasant experience, and your coach is not there to entertain you. At some point you will doubtless feel resentment towards them, but remember that anything you feel towards them is simply a reflection of what you are feeling towards yourself: for example, if they say something that annoys you, it probably means that they have struck a nerve. A good coach leads their client towards autonomy and independence. You should never become dependent on your sessions – quite the opposite.

Finding the right coach is like shopping for a new pair of shoes: you might have to try ten on before finding a pair that fit you. Before deciding whether or not to keep a coach on, analyse your own reaction to them. Why do they annoy you? Why do you feel uncomfortable? Do they seem too confident or too aloof? Each meeting will help you to refine your requirements and help you with your search.

TOP TIPS

- Define your goals before you begin your search, or you may not choose the coach who is best suited to your needs.
- Use word of mouth to help you make your decision. You will be quicker to trust someone who has been recommended to you.
- Training does not a good coach make, even though it is an important factor to consider. Having a massive variety of tools at your disposal is pointless if you do not know how to use them and adapt them to the needs of each individual patient. Do not let yourself be dazzled by a CV that is bursting with qualifications, and pay attention to their personal experience instead.
- Do not let yourself be limited by geography. Sometimes, the ideal coach for you may be based a little further away, but you should not let that stop you, especially if your first meeting is promising. Nowadays, many specialists also work via video calls or by telephone. If you are comfortable with these methods, the

quality of your coaching will not suffer.

- Do not hesitate to ask your coach about their methods, their past experiences, or how their sessions work – it is important to find out if their style will suit you or not.
- Take your personality and your coach's personality into account. A good connection between client and coach is the deciding factor in the success of the coaching process. Above all, trust your intuition. If you have an interview with someone who fits all the criteria you are looking for, but something does not feel right, listen to your instincts. If you do not feel comfortable with them, the coaching will not be effective.
- Your coach should go at your pace and adapt their approach according to your needs. Do not hesitate to tell them if you are struggling and to ask them to slow down if necessary.

FAQS

WILL AN OLDER COACH BE MORE QUALIFIED THAN SOMEONE YOUNGER?

The most persistent myth about coaching suggests that a coach's quality is dictated by the number of wrinkles they have. Do not be fooled – age is no guarantee. A good coach is defined by the quality of their guidance, their ability to support and listen to their clients, and their training: any coach, regardless of their age, will learn new things every day and will be continually improving thanks to their clients. Of course, experience plays an important role in coaching, but it is more important that your coach uses it to help you move forward.

DOES MY SUCCESS DEPEND ENTIRELY ON MY COACH?

Naturally, whether or not you achieve your goals will depend on both you and your coach.

Your coach will suggest exercises for you to do between sessions and information for you to look up, and will use all the methods at their disposal to help you to achieve your goal, but you are the only one who can determine the outcome. Everything depends on how you engage with the coaching process. Your coach is there to motivate you and to monitor your progress, but they cannot do things for you. You are the only one who can write your own story.

WHAT ARE THE DIFFERENCES BETWEEN A COACH, A COUNSELLOR AND A THERAPIST?

Unlike a counsellor, who focuses on a situation which is causing problems and tries to help you find solutions, a coach is interested in you as a person. They will give you potential leads to follow, open your mind, make you aware of alternative perspectives, challenge you to change your outlook, and so on. They will never offer you magic solutions based on subjective advice. If you feel that your coach is trying to force their own opinion or their own vision for your future upon you, do not hesitate to transfer to someone else.

Furthermore, although the coaching profession has evolved a great deal, it remains very distinct from therapy. Coaching is very action-oriented, whereas therapy is more dialogue-focused. However, the two are not incompatible, so do not hesitate to seek both at the same time. In fact, this strategy can prove highly effective, as the coaching process can dredge up certain psychological wounds which will then slow down your progress. Talking to a therapist about them will help you to stay on track.

CAN ANYONE BECOME A COACH?

In theory, anyone can claim to be a coach even if they have absolutely no training because it is not a licensed profession, and no particular qualifications are required to practise. Licensed professions are regulated by law, which means that you can be prosecuted for practising them without suitable qualifications. However, there are no legal measures that you can resort to if you encounter a fraud masquerading as a coach, so it is important to be vigilant. However, you should also remember that the quality of a coach does not necessarily depend on their training.

WHAT QUALITIES DOES AN EFFECTIVE COACH NEED?

You can identify a good coach by keeping an eye out for certain attitudes. Among others, these should include:

- the willingness to listen, without blindly agreeing with everything you say;
- the ability to challenge you in a constructive manner so that you do not get off-track;
- a knack for asking the right questions, meaning the kind of questions that will make you think and grow;
- the humility to focus exclusively on their client;
- a focus on making you more independent instead of creating a dependence on your sessions with them;
- continued training.

WILL IT BE VERY EXPENSIVE TO HIRE A GOOD COACH?

This is a difficult question, because it depends. The word "expensive" means very different things to different people, and drastically different price brackets can work better for different people. Decide on a budget, as this will help you to make your choice. Also, bear in mind that an expensive coach will not necessarily be better than a more affordable one, and vice versa.

HOW CAN I SPOT A BAD COACH?

- They try to sell you a fantasy and promise to change your life. Of course, coaching can do that, but only if you are equally committed. Your coach cannot make those changes happen by themselves.
- They judge you, criticise you, and hurl accusations at you.
- They think they are better than you and try to adopt a superior or even dominating attitude towards you.
- They confuse coaching with marketing, meaning that they try to sell you all kinds of other products (seminars, books, methods, etc.) instead of concentrating on the guidance you need.

OVER TO YOU

Try using this short list of questions as a starting point for choosing a coach who suits you:

- What kind of coaching are you looking for? Is it related to your career, your family, your personal life, your relationships, or your health? This will help you to figure out what type of coach you need.
- What are your real needs? Use your answer to this question to clarify what is essential to you and what your demands are.
- What qualities and values do you want your coach to have? Make a list and compare it with the coaches you meet and the information provided on their websites.
- Would you be more comfortable with a man or a woman?
- What budget can you set aside for your coaching?

We want to hear from you!
Leave a comment on your online library
and share your favourite books on social media!

FURTHER READING

BIBLIOGRAPHY

- Cannio, S. and Launer, V. (2009) *Le métier de coach. Cas de coaching commentés.* Paris: Éditions Eyrolles.

- Journal du Net. (2007) Les clés pour bien choisir son coach. [Online]. [Accessed 18 October 2017]. Available from: <http://www.journaldunet.com/management/dossiers/040745coaching/conseils-pour-choisir.shtml>

IMPROVE YOUR GENERAL KNOWLEDGE

IN A BLINK OF AN EYE !

www.50minutes.com